EVE NAMES THE ANIMALS

The Morse Poetry Prize
Edited by Guy Rotella

SUSAN DONNELLY

Eve Names the Animals

THE 1984 MORSE
POETRY PRIZE
☙ SELECTED AND
INTRODUCED BY
ANTHONY HECHT

Northeastern University Press
BOSTON

Designer: Ann Twombly

Northeastern University Press
Copyright © 1985 by Susan Donnelly

Library of Congress Cataloging in Publication Data

Donnelly, Susan, 1939–
   Eve names the animals.
   I. Hecht, Anthony, 1923–   . II. Title.
PS3554.O533E8   1984   811'.54   84-16714
ISBN 0-930350-64-2

Composed in Weiss by Monotype Composition,
Baltimore, Maryland. Printed and bound at the Alpine
Press, Stoughton, Massachusetts. The paper is Warren's
No. 66 Antique, an acid-free sheet.

MANUFACTURED IN THE UNITED STATES OF AMERICA
90   89   88   87   86   85   5   4   3   2   1

For my parents: Francis and Mary Higgins

ACKNOWLEDGMENTS

The poems in this book have appeared in the following magazines: *The Beloit Poetry Journal* ("Eve Names the Animals"); *The Boston Monthly* ("Ark Song," "Dolls," "In Purcell's Cafeteria Off Pi Alley," "On Discovering a Poem by My Great-Uncle Will Leahy"); *Dark Horse* ("Body," "Naiad Speaks"); *Ploughshares* ("That Time, That Country," "The House of My Birth," "A Little Cloud," "Painting of a Woman with Vines"); *Poetry Northwest* ("In Her Dream"); *Shadowgraphs* ("Constellation" under the name of "The Dead Girl," "Landscape with Family," "Legend," "Nana," "When I Couldn't Afford Poetry"); *Sojourner* ("Aunt," "To My Ear"); *Soundings East* ("Landscape," "Making Love to the Milkman," "The Summer Clothes Curse," "The Apple Tree," "Moving Day"); and *Yankee* ("The Week Before I Was Born").

"Constellation" and "Eve Names the Animals" appeared in *Saturday's Women* (Saturday Press, 1982).

"The Rooms" won second prize in the 1983 Billee Murray Denny poetry contest and was published in 1984 in the contest book.

"Rilke Speaks of Angels" was published in 1984 in *Milkweed Chronicle*'s anthology, *The Poet Dreaming in the Artist's House.*

Contents

Introduction

Young poets very often resemble an enthusiastic and grateful twelve-year-old who has been given a kit of magic tricks for Christmas. With enormous zeal, and somewhat less patience, he goes off to learn and rehearse his skills, and in two weeks summons his family excitedly to witness a demonstration of his art just after dinner. His grandmother is prepared to admire anything he does, no matter how clumsy; his parents have put on fixed smiles and do not expect any miracles; and his older brother presents a bare mastery of boredom. The first trick involves making a Kennedy half-dollar disappear into thin air, and then astonishingly retrieving it from behind his grandmother's ear. This is saluted with genuine and enthusiastic applause, having been brought off very smoothly, along with some diverting patter. But it then appears that this is the only trick that young Mandrake, in his impatience to become an admired performer, has mastered; and when urged by his approving audience to continue, he is somewhat awkwardly obliged to do the same trick again. As a trick it is not unimpressive; not everyone can do it. But the older brother's worst fears are grimly confirmed, and he finds a fairly transparent reason to excuse himself from the room, even though, or especially because, grandmother is prepared to serve as an endless source, a veritable mint, of Kennedy half-dollars.

The young poet has usually worked his way through all manner of difficulties before achieving what he wants to call "a voice of his own"; by which he is likely to mean an idiom that is paradoxically both natural and strange. It should be "natural" in the sense of being unforced by the contingencies of poetic necessity; that is to say, its mode of speech should present a consistent context for any extravagance it cares to entertain. It should, on the other hand, be "strange" in at least the sense that it offers the reader, as Mandrake offers his family, something that they were not exactly expecting: a certain mastery, a smoothness, even a casualness that disarms, and allows the surprise to seem to happen all of its own accord. And having learned this initial skill (which costs far more discipline, labor, and frustration than any non-poet or non-magician could guess), he finds himself at last able to write about a lot of things in what amounts to an earned formula, a diction that serves as his persona, his stage-presence. And there are not a few poets, some of them, alas, quite celebrated, who relax into this early-acquired posture, and proceed to turn out reams and volumes that are indistinguishable from one another.

All the manuscripts I considered were submitted anonymously, and so I had no knowledge whatever of the identity of the poet whose excellent volume, *Eve Names the Animals*, I have chosen. But internal evidence strongly suggested that the poet is a woman and one at the beginning of her writing career. What seems to me to be the conspicuous merit of this collection consists in its splendid wit, its daring, its copiousness of invention, and its not infrequent sprightliness. The poet—I now know her to be Susan Donnelly— has found a way to speak not merely in her own poetic voice, but has been able to give voice to other people as well, and even to inanimate things. She has Emily Dickinson's cryptic sense of playful and serious riddle, and she animates even the most inert features of the world around her. She has not, in other words, settled for a few selected parlor tricks, but has moved out into a world more diverse, more unexpected than most young poets are able to engage or command. I presume to think of Ms. Donnelly as young in terms of poetry because her poems are not uniformly excellent. She has so fertile and prolific a fund of metaphoric language that it sometimes gets out of hand, and she allows her rich capacity for invention to mislead her. This is the sort of fault I find not only easy but agreeable to indulge, and even more to admire in a certain way, though it is one she will have to learn to keep an eye on. But her work presents a density and energy of imagination that strikes me as so strong that I am delighted to have been given the chance to make her literary acquaintance, and to award her the Morse Poetry Prize.

ANTHONY HECHT

PART I

A Door Marked Permission

✒ The Week Before I Was Born

It was Indian summer.
Tomatoes split on the vines
in the shaggy garden.

When my mother walked, music
filled me. Sounds
I couldn't resist.
Thoughts flowed in and out of my eyes,
and I slept.

But when she slept,
I sported.
I was a tightrope dancer,
skilled in the free fall.

She gets up for a drink of water,
rubs her back. My father
squeezes his eyes shut.

She looks out over the garden
where a cat, or a rabbit,
changes the shape of the dark.

The moon climbs,
shaking off clouds that would hold it.

Everything beneath it seems about to speak.

✌ Eve Names the Animals

To me, *lion* was sun on a wing
over the garden. *Dove*,
a burrowing, blind creature.

I swear that man
never knew animals. Words
he lined up according to size,

while elephants slipped flat-eyed
through water

and trout
hurtled from the underbrush, tusked
and ready for battle.

The name he gave me stuck
me to him. He did it to comfort me,
for not being first.

Mornings, while he slept,
I got away. Pickerel
hopped on the branches above me.
Only spider accompanied me,

nosing everywhere,
running up to lick my hand.

Poor finch. I suppose I was
woe to him—

the way he'd come looking for me,
not wanting either of us
to be ever alone.

But to myself I was
palomino
      raven
            fox . . .

I strung words
by their stems and wore them
as garlands on my long walks.

The next day
I'd find them withered.

I liked change.

꧁ To My Ear

Do you hear me? I say you are wonderful
the way you forget and the way you recall.
How you suck in the most flotsam compliment,
vain shell, then clamp shut like a bivalve
at the wrong truths. Listen, I mean you well.

It's true that I had hoped for something
a little more, shall I say, audible?
after that moondeaf walk when he and I
stumbled up words. You were my tape cassette,
your spindles quivering. I left it up to you.

Listen, the Marriage of Figaro still enters
chiming. The right key turns in the lock.
Meat sizzles, water sports over rocks,
loons brood on Damariscotta and
you are there, receiver. Listen.

In Her Dream

A baby cries in my mother's midnight,
cries for food from the lost chamber,

summons her, a towhead girl, from dreams
of her childhood on Laurel Street. Upstairs

in the room she has always suspected,
the baby wrings itself out with wailing.

The cry pulls great ribbony swathes
from my mother's chest: bunting,

grosgrain, pink satin blanket edging,
toddler harness strings, birthday ribbon,

the brittle cinnamon folds
of Christmas candy. Slowly her hair

turns grey, the blue-green eyes rheum
with uncertainty. At last, a vein part crimson,

part silver unwinds from her. This
is the skein we were not to touch,

the look-away skein none of us
dragged from her—none but that howler.

And how could a child be forgotten
so long in the last nursery?

She walks up the stairs. Below her,
school chums catch rubber balls

to their chests. Their jump-rope confidence
falters. "Mary! Mary!" The steps

are so difficult. Sea grass like cats' tongues.
Above, the mew-cry circling.

At the top of the stairs she pauses.
Her father, his baldness hidden

by Irish linen, studies cormorants
through field glasses. Her brothers pose

in a bony pyramid, then capsize
on the sand. The beach makes its grand gestures.

And the cunning mosquito nags
into her mind's tunnels,

hungry for brain. The cry,
the cry. She comes to a door marked "PERMISSION"

in curled blue letters. The door
is a blackened mirror, a silver rot

of fish scales, mica, kelp and
smashed baby-pink crabshells. "I'm coming."

The crib cave beckons. Veins scrawl
inside the transparent skull. But the baby

holds up two fingers, in a china Christ's
pretty blessing. Its smock covers air.

The cheeks are moonpits of hunger.
My mother becomes a well

the moon may dip into forever,
always drawing up salt.

The baby shrinks to a wish-coin in her hand.

The Apple Tree

I was as full of spring
as any around me.
I heard the calf-song.
When bees philandered
from one to another,

we shivered and drew our petals
around us, fluttering them like fans.

Were all our frivolities,
the drum of July beating louder
and at night, crickets
shrilling eagerly like old wives,

only to fatten
these glistening bold ones
who roll off into the waiting grass
to be bruised and forgotten,

or gathered, crushed
and their sweet
juices drawn from them?

The dances we did
in the night meadow! Yes,
I was ripe for the red season.

Now I repeat to myself
the lesson of stillness,

while over the fields
come the ice daughters
sowing their glittery seeds.

﹏ Cassandra

When you left us, Cassandra,
we saw each other again.

Into the rooms came sun
like a whiskbroom. Moles,

crooked teeth, palms full of light,
laps like bowls of herbs,

the backs of necks where the smell
lingered, of cigarettes and sleep.

When you left, wearing
your bruised cloak, the house

took up its whileaway tune.
Trees stroked it, lilacs stirred

like tousled heads. A child
lay watching the ceiling's mane,

saw the flung-out triumph
of a boy rider. Elsewhere, a room's

petals revealed a deep,
carnelian center. If you had asked,

we would have said: we close
our eyes and our bodies open.

But your blunt fingers thundered
all down the lefthand keyboard.

The house lay in a shroud
you tore from stormclouds,

your dark purple eyes
full of a rage of candor.

Cassie. Ten years old,
you strode ahead of me,

warning of gypsies. Bushes
scratched our tough summer legs.

How they brewed up potions
from dandelion greens,

how they kidnapped children,
blew them from home like white seeds.

Their bitter drink made people talk,
made them tell all. "But,"

you said, "I'll protect you."
One hand neatly split

a cattail leaf. Its life-juice
shone under your nail.

I dream we row in a pod boat.
Evenly. Each of us holds an oar.

On the bank, shapes appear. Mother
bends like a willow. A man, a child.

You see them. Frantically
spin the boat, drawing it downward.

But didn't you know I was one of them?

II. CASSANDRA ANSWERS:

You wear your pride
like a sundress, Laurie—

a soft thing, easily shucked off.
You touch your husband's shoulder.

But he's no talisman. And Mother,
collecting her tansy and pennywort—

flowers so common
they don't need names.

That whole house is open
to any weather. Each year

the paint curls off, as the mist
moves closer. At night,

when the blind rattles the window,
you pretend you don't hear.

Telling ever-after stories
so the child shivers

deliciously, leans his head
against you. What I saw

you refused. Always.
I watched the nursery paint glass

cloud, streak with yellow
like heat lightning.

You painted your stick family
going in at their gate.

I tell you,
there was no safety

in Mother smoothing our hair,
in curtains idling

at summer windows. The world
is a place where every second

some child vanishes.
You know this, Laurie.

Only by pressing my fingers
against my eyelids

can I see your way:
a slow gold rising through darkness.

✺ Constellation

Although the stranger dragged me from my car,
I am not robbed
of my lover's smell or touch
nor of the arch of colors
when he moves inside me.

Although I screamed up the deaf street,
my friends Betsy and Jane
laugh with me
around my kitchen table
and the jealous cat
creeps up
to warm my lap.

Although the abandoned house had doom eyes
and the graffiti mocked me,
my mother
teaches me the names of flowers,
splitting milkweed pods
so that their silver abundance
lightens the air.

Although he tore off my clothes,
Sister Theresa Mary
hands me the Latin prize.
I see dust
puff from the crimson
auditorium curtain.

Although he beat me to the ground
and that room stank
of ash and urine
and dead animals,
my grandfather calls me
Pixie.

From the back lawn after supper
he shows me
Cassiopeia
and the Hunter
who move as we move.

Although the thuds,
the panting
and pig squeals that came from me
enclosed a deep silence,
pieces of moments
tumble smooth for me
like all the mauve and brown pebbles
gathered on Nauset Beach.

~ Body

Patient dreamer.

All winter
as my footsteps
froze behind me
and I followed the sad agendas
you were alive.

Sometimes I was sure
you had become like the starved earth.
That I had taken January
into myself, a loveless marriage.

But you'd send out
puffs of hope with my breath,
telling me: I am still warm.

Body, you have no pride.
You'd let any June breeze
part your legs—
a Beaux Arts trio
or a sailor breeze
hot from the subway grating.

You're sanguine. Even trite.
At night your guerilla band
overturns my dreams.

Then we wake
and you bounce like a paddleball
on its short-lived elastic.

What do you care?
Spring. Spring again.

✍ The Summer Clothes Curse

She's betrayed us! She knows
the very ripple and stroke
of our weave against her thighs,

the droop of us on the bed
waiting for evening.

She knows the way we keep
perfume, cigarettes,
the odor of love inside us.

We protect her.
Catch on the odd nail
as she heads toward danger.
Preserve the lost months: crushed
straw hat, sandals
with her toes' imprint.

But she shuts us
into this closet,
where midwinter sags
like a rope bridge. We

who love release—
zippers opening gladly,
tenderness
rustling down into a heap.

Let her become a snow-woman,
melting only to death.
Chickadees,
pester her. Let her be seen

from the back, where she's dumpy.
Fix her eyes northward.
May they glint

like coal chips no fire consumes.
May her arms become
torn off branches
whose sap is arrested forever.

At the end of each arm
hang a mitten.
Let the thumbs freeze shut.

༄ *Naiad Speaks*

Paralyzed with the cold she was saved
by a man, but had to be hospitalized for
the burns left by his 98.6° hands.
—from a *New York Times* article
  about marathon swimmer Diana Nyad

Prince of the mean
so ravishingly normal
you grew. Your shoulders
broadened on cue
and you bought
a wrist corsage
of rosebuds
for your prom queen.

I waited in the sea cave.
Seaweed inside me
like stalactites
or a shiver.
So frozen in my attitude
I'd forgotten temperature.
My skin strange
as Alonso's. Bones
clattering like clamshells
spat onto rocks
by hungry gulls.
My aurora borealis—
the green sun
seen through fathoms.

Noontime:
handsome and fit
in your wet suit

with your scuba certificate
you thrust the
tiresome waves apart
like pushing through crowds.

You smile,
check your equipment
and plummet straight to me.

98.6

I burn alive.

Making Love to the Milkman

He's predictable.
Yet with that shock

of red hair
my son is known by.

I don't trust a man
in a closed van. Give me

a butter-colored truck,
Guernsey in watercress,
laid back door

and him swinging out
in the quickmarch
of the deliverer.

None of your waxy
cardboard.
He brings bottles

trembling together, dewed
with early morning,

and feathered brown eggs
that fit your palm. His

is Grade A
sun, tempered
so you can look
straight at it,

distillation of meadow
blown from the pod
in a lavish scattering,

cream
rising to the top
of the daily churn.

Human kindness.

✒ Ark Song

Come, my beloved, while the storm
creates asymmetry out of form.

Over us ocean, beneath us sky.
The rising waters like clouds move by.

Trees become islands, desert beach.
Then follow the animals as each,

led by defaulting fate above,
picks an unlawful mate to love.

The agile monkey woos the bear.
The ocelot sighs in the panther's lair.

The elephant sinks to his knees. His ears
flutter with wren sounds, which he hears

like the wind in the grasses under the sea.
—And your cool breath rekindles me.

Radiant Scripture we shall learn
on dark hay stored in creaking stern

where we, though landsmen find it shocking,
match the Ark's roll with our own rocking,

while at the bow of our walnut shell,
the lion fondles his sweet gazelle.

~ Moving Day

If I remembered which box held the spoons I'd set
myself breakfast. I nest wherever I find myself—
cup, orange, book alongside, salt and pepper guarding
my place like parents: Mum who heightened the ordinary,
Dad tossing on warnings so I sneezed in mid-adventure.
Both packed away now with the slotted spoon I'd love
to hold over each box, drawing out the frilled, shaking
white, the yolk solid and smiling as a grocer. From
one box, nail polish ether. I watch Aunt Bea clench her
fingers, then hold them out in a lovely gesture. Syringa
mixes its scent with the polish; Bea's hand disperses
sundust. In another box, essence of women friends:
quiche at rickety tables, loyal rampages against the man,
letters signed 'much love' chatting even as they ride
in the mailman's pouch. But here I'm Primavera, with
no nymphs tripping a welcome. I've worn the same dress
all my life. Its dacron flowers cluster at breast,
at crotch. If I scuffled around for cover, would I
find a fur collar from a flea market? A rubber boot?
You said no one could pack enough for all weathers.
But you were my weatherman. I watched you for
storms, for the falling glass. In your balmy days,
I packed picnics. The night we ended it I toyed with
an enamelled box. Its top fit only one way. A ring,
a key, a blue marble. I tried on the ring, felt the key's
groove, saw our words enter the marble, dizzy themselves
in its pattern. Now clouds scoff at marble. The blue
sky leads outward. I open the window, sit down on the
nearest box. I won't unpack yet.

✍ In Purcell's Cafeteria Off Pi Alley

You've got to know what you want and talk fast.
There's a rhythm you've got to pick up
like a plate passing quickly from hand
to hand, your demand for corned beef
on rye with a pickle or salad
with feta, black olives and oil,
or one slice of meatloaf with mashed
then Sprite Pepsi Fanta or Tab
coffee black or whatever's on tap.

You've got to know what you ordered and grab.
There's a grace to the slide of the plate
over counters, the nod, the exchange,
jostled arms reaching out for the change.
(You've staked out your table beforehand,
now you bodycheck over with tray.)
Near the door a large landscape of Maine
hangs crooked, a gesture toward nature
with pine trees and deer and a sunset.
The noontimers crowd in and out,
each gust of the city bestowing
on the idyll a little more grime
and all the Thoreaus tap their drumbeats
on the tables marked Sandwich Time.

To men, the city's a given.
It's just what the world is—foundation
executives, errand boys, lawyers,
trust officers, truckers, or bums.
They know it is real, they move fast,
they've ordered before, they've been pushed,
they have their change ready, they shrug
off the jumble, to them the air
normal as Monday, the Red Sox, Dow Jones.

I move in the city with daring
delight, its grey air a charge
of sexual energy, breathtaking, breezy.
Skirt blowing, quickening heartbeat.
As the doors of Purcell's swing open
the clamor envelops me. Trembling,
an old man eats custard and winks.
The bag lady names me her heiress.

I'm a child, they have just let me out
of my yard. I've discovered the treasure.
I am shaking it, listening, holding it up
so the light glances off it.
I could wear it, could eat it
(one steak and cheese on a sub).
It is my Hub, my city,
my racket and stink and high motion.
I know what I want and hold fast.
My short order—to stay or to go.

The Poem's Effect on Harvard Square

None. The kid still shoves you
a pass to 33 Dunster. Sign up

to vote. Or stick with a flyer
the rooters for Harvard

when the bloody band
flows home. Cranes

guard the slurry trenches.
Fleas peddle earrings.

A dubious incense rises. Lifts
the new eyebrows of teens

who dip nipples at
lonesome priests. Cooped

in a doorway:
a huddle of violins

and a hat. No one's
listening. Everyone's

crossing. Waiting. Starting
a date. Words

are licked jimmies.
Shot on a melting cone.

When I Couldn't Afford Poetry

closetful of words   heaped up
ready for Goodwill
on the refrigerator door
the list grows longer
ketchup-spattered
words
I would have written

prose stalks me   interrupted
at every turn of phrase
garrulous bills
kids' teeth
supporting the receptionist
Master Charged conscience
prodding me awake
heavy with words

breasts aching
full of words
sunnyblooming wine days
becoming
headaches

whole cumulus stanzas
escaping through the blue sky
no ballads
in the crowds today
no lyric glances
certainly no epics in the *Globe*

back home
speechless with good sense
words
hustled into dustpans   words
clogging the drains

and always
waiting   waiting
three dumb notebooks
pages smooth   pointless
as storefresh Wamsutta
percale
nobody's rolled in

Dolls

Maidy was pretty and empty-headed,
wore a black uniform with a white frill.
A flighty blonde, tactless, well-bedded.
Lightsome meddler with strong men's will.

Mother was steady, dressed in a scrap of brown
checked gingham from our mother's apron.
Her arms stuck out, her mouth was a snap
of putty good sense, her eyes like raisins.

As for Father, his haberdasher
has dressed him in tan felt, a smudge of tie,
brown painted hair and a tremor of rashness,
despite good citizenship, in one blue eye.

He's upstairs shaving, in painful posture,
stiffly leaned against the bathroom wall.
The wavering mirror reveals an imposter
as Maidy's song torments from the hall.

A family man, from a clothespin bed
where with dull Mother he begets kewpies,
he's now spring-fevered out of his head,
ready to leap from his tintown duties.

Suddenly he stammers his declaration,
clumsy and ardent before the maid.
We awkwardly entwine them. Then, impatient,
turn to the everyday dolls outside.

But Maidy's fickle. Soon she yawns
and flounces away for a date with a bruiser.
Mother sees where Father has gone
over the sofa-mountains, a loser

who falls on his own from the crewel pillow,
forgotten by us, chewed by the basset.
Which calls for an occasion of funeral thrill,
a spoon-dug grave and a cardboard casket.

Now Maidy whistles her randy ditty,
her bold eyes wink at the glare of spring.
But Mother wonders, in fear and pity,
if large, careless hands control everything.

✤ The Winter We Made Bread

The winter we made bread
was our sixteenth year together.

We need more
loaf pans. We need
a brioche pan, you said,
thumbing through
Breads of the World
as I pulled on an old sweater
and creamed my face
with Oil of Olay, for bed.

> Finnish rye
> was our debut—
> its orange rind sharp,
> unexpected
> in the workaday dark dough.

Next baking day
I got up early
from where we lay rounded
back to back, warm
as loaves
to savor
a treacherous dream . . .

The dream man
followed me
to the bright kitchen
where your list waited
under the bottle of
Chateau Lascombes Margaux
we'd expanded with
the night before,
boring our adolescents

with our fervor
as we leaned towards each other
over the wax-spattered table.

    Cumin, the list read,
    fennel,
    anise
    and buttermilk
    for Surmjölksbröd.

        Old friend,

that hungry couple
in the gourmet guide
knew a lot,
but not our recipes.

When you flipped over
the frying English muffins
we saw
their perfect freckles.

I know you sat up alone
past midnight
eating them. I know
you smoked too much.

Did you know
the foolish yeast
that rose in me?

✺ Landscape

I.

I stand here
clear-etched
as a pioneer woman
trapped in a monument.

Low tide
ripens Moody's Creek,
poking up rocks
like the hairy heads of trolls.

Beyond them
was Emma Parmelee's house.

      Now it's a trashed lot.

Goldenrod,
Queen Anne's lace,
a foundation like old teeth,
where somebody's slungbellied
cat picks her way,
nosing at fishcans.

When they smashed Emma's walls,
the sprigged wallpaper
and yellow stains by the radiator
made you look away.

Now the lot waits
for the tin boxes
we villagers favor.
Mobile homes
like cold storage vaults and

wacky-winged

duck weathervanes
that never catch up.

"We villagers." Listen to me.
Westchester girl.
Askance, now,
as any native.

II.

Rob and I
came here in '68.
The closer you got
to salt, the further
Sirhan, Chicago, the flaming jelly
that clung to newsprint.

We hid that winter.
Holed up in one room.
When the Franklin stove
glowed to a pitch,
I'd throw off the quilt
and he'd cover me.

Pearled clouds
rushed past the moon in the kitchen window.
            We chuckled,
like children playing sardines.

Next spring, our hopes
were tomato plants.

We were hellbent
on innocence.
The red juice
spilling over our fingers.

III.

Rob is drawn
to the city.

It's gradual.
        The tide,
leaving the beach,
comes back to reassure shells.

Yet his sandprints are empty.

He's off in the morning,
smelling of money.   A golden
wrist shoots from a cuff,
checks the time.

                His gears
no longer fit mine.

The works of some
small, ticking office woman
engage him.

I try to imagine their time.
Or not to imagine it.

The kitchen faucet
weeps. When he comes home
at nine, his headlights
are falling stars.

The kids glance up
        from television,
expecting nothing.

IV.

There is in me some refusal
to make a fuss.

Anne Rogers:
    sleeves rolled up,
            dark yellow hair
tucked away. Everything stray
tucked away. Rob,

see past my face!

I am eel grass, steeped
in the regular wash
of the tide.

            I'm a sunflower.
I smile, when the crownheaded
scarlet cardinals fly off
with my seeds.

I hear the whippoorwill
cry death

            death

    if we leave here.

Who will pierce me?

This mouth could soften.

            My mouths
            could be wet—

Believe me,
they could engulf
even the salt Atlantic.

37

⫸ That Time, That Country

In the country that was a time
I spoke in tongues,

a glossolalia of joy, like birdsong
in Beethoven's Sixth.

It was March in that country.
At the sign of the Lamb and Lion,

a chambermaid flings open a window.
That was the time

I shed the baggage
of extra flesh, to feel

frankness on my arms
that had been so wooden.

I forgave my city its grey
walls, shadows and gilt, bodies

rippling on the plateglass of stores.
For I saw him everywhere,

taking the form of strangers.
I came to believe

in corners, for what might lie
around them. What did I heed,

then, of the sad rush under my feet
as I watched carpets shaken from high windows

like flags of state? And saw even doormen
look up at the cry of wild geese

beating their way northward?
A flower cart

stood at the curb, filled
with the crayon colors of childhood.

My countrymen opened to me
their individual faces. As for the sky,

it had the look of the past
but it shimmered with news.

PART II

Coral Builders in the Sea of Time

◀ The House of My Birth

A flotilla of ceilings
moves like gulls over the drowned

faces of ancestors. In a garden of shells,
Kitty, my great-grandmother,

plays a coral pianoforte.
Her black curls, "beau-catchers,"

flutter with every current.
The carpets give up their ghosts.

All the eccentric corners
hold uncles, ginger-haired, twisting

pouches of tobacco. The sachet aunts
are tucked into oak and cherry.

Missals lie heaped on the hall table,
their silk snake tongues

marking penance and Pentecost.
The weighted grandfather

clock descends through each week
with his gold burdens. I hear an

alto-soprano of daughters
doing the Sunday dishes:

"Over the Ocean Columbus Came."
They plunge their hands wrist-deep

into suds like trousseau lace.
A flicker of nightfall

darkens their faces. I see the glow
behind skin as it waits

with a candle. Then each sister
enters her own castle. One is hidden

by sea urchins. One trails
her long green hair

like moss from a window. A third,
my namesake,

climbs to the tower of bone.
What is darkness,

what is light? she sings. And above her
the family motto:

    Amor et silentium.

On Discovering a Poem By My Great-Uncle Will Leahy in an Antique Shop in Kennebunkport

You wrote of stars and oceans, grandly.
Your spirit "a wild sea-bird." Who were you,
whose only outward mourning was clenched hands
when illness kept you from your mother's funeral?
Lover of Audubon, Harvard, classics and Cathleen-
ni-Houlihan, but no real Southie girl.
You wrote of death, were not much more than twenty
when *Scribner's* set you next to Henry James.

Uncle, you held me once. You catch me now
sunburned and lazy, browsing among butterchurns.
A wild bird, exulting over Kennebunk,
cries out this find, this flight between us.
I read your words and write. We're kinfolk.
"poor coral builders in the sea of time."

‮≋‬ Nana

You were like a flower.
A carnation.
Your spicy sweetness
reflected in your puns,
a certain tartness.
You told me stories about bad Lucy
as you sat mending
in the shaded bedroom.
The neat complexities
of your wicker sewing basket
lured me into the story.
Then you snipped the thread,
wound up the moral.

Your hats were important.
Each spring Miss Dixon
would produce the straw with flowers,
tasteful, gay
and slightly different from the year before.
As though, in a handkerchief garden,
you would dare
one different flower—
cyclamen perhaps.

Mornings your telephone
was the center of a web
of daughterly chats,
domestic gossamer,
the kitchen gardens
of their lives
tended before your eyes.
Though what they did
you thought too arduous,
foolish, almost

unladylike.
You were anxious
at their good health,
your blood pressure fluttering
at the energies of the new age.

In your world
a lady
dealt with S. S. Pierce on the telephone,
made half a bed
with strapping Irish girls,
tripped into town to shop,
breathed decorously
the subtle fragrance
of dewy infants.

When I was eight
and gruesome with chicken pox
you brought me a potted plant.
Sue-bird, you called me.
Pert, never praising,
your head tipped to one side.
Handsome is as handsome does
you'd say, if called to compliment.

At the ocean—how we would laugh!
You wore shoes into the water. Rubber shoes!
Full of graceful fear
at the immensities of the Atlantic.

Remember when you'd brush
your long rippled greying hair
and we'd stand laughing round you?
Old witch! Old witch!
we'd cry tenderly

and you'd wind it up, snap
the elastics, fix it with tortoise shell,
smiling at your reflection
between the curtseying Doulton ladies.

Dear Nana,
one picture shows you at a wedding,
jaunty and shy,
as you stroll beside blooming Papa
down Chestnut Hill Avenue.
In another, a snapshot,
you stand on a verandah
before a screen door in Hull,
holding out a bunch of flowers
in summer greeting.

Seeing you there,
I put aside
the querulous frailty of your last weeks
when your color and your fragrance faded.
I approach gently,
as along a flagged and winding path,
to touch you with my words—

A child's finger in the mouth of a snapdragon.
The feel of its delicate bite.

◕ Aunt

She runs onto the porch in a whirl of skirts.
Filigree-held, like a fish in a bowl.
A locket opens. It is Fourth of July.
Whom does she seek on the white beach road?

Filigree-held, like a fish in a bowl.
Behind her the roast beef, mahogany air.
Whom does she seek on the white beach road?
Mama is whaleboned to a straightback chair.

Behind her the roast beef, mahogany air.
She is redgold, thrashing. Circle on a chain.
Mama whaleboned to a straightback chair.
Daughter then mother then daughter again.

Redgold, thrashing. Circle on a chain.
She runs onto the porch in a whirl of skirts.
Daughter then mother then daughter again.
A locket opens. It is Fourth of July.

৶ A Little Cloud

The cloud is a bowler hat,
a profile delicate and handsome,
a cane,

a figure falling,
the plume of smoke from a train.

My grandfather
sits up straight,
his dark eyebrows rakish
and innocent.

The hooded photographer
shoots his plates
back and forth.

The cloud becomes
a pigeon's wing. Caught
in four o'clock

November sadness,
the young man hunches,
Cratchit-like
over his ledgers,

forcing a steady Palmer
from the hand that already
trembles with chorea.

At six o'clock
the cloud conducts him
along Boston's cow paths,
dense with provincial importance,
to the train.

Inside Mulcahy's

a froth of conversation spills
over the sides of mugs.

Grandfather
shrugs, puns, draws cartoons
in the creamy splash

while, in the bar mirror,
an ironic angel with dark eyebrows
tips its hat, presents him
the usual bill:

the kitchen falling
into a faint, his blazing wife
and in the doorway

the nightshirted
six-year-old
clutching his sex for comfort.

And I wait inside the boy
for my own beginnings.
I store it all:

that harrowing,
humor tossed like change
on the counter, the self-
salute in the mirror.

The cloud
fills my greenhouse
with a fragrance
of loam. Vines

stretch to the highest frames
as the soft rain
mouths on the glass.

﹏ The Rooms

1. GUEST ROOM

I smell of camphor. My sheets precise, windows revealing
forgotten angles of garden. A wallflower of a room,
closets swinging with prom dresses and dead men's suits.
But under my beds are excellent hiding places. I eavesdrop
the nine year old's caught breath and drumming shoes.
Few guests, though the woman irons finger towels, smooths
a bedspread. And when they do threaten, I pick up her
anxiety like the smell of rainclouds, hear her mutter
as she struggles to rid the curtains of my mild dust.
At last she lies down on the near bed. I draw silken
shadows up the walls. Rest, I tell her, where your
daughter diaried her blue and gold secrets. Your lost
baby brother slept here, for one night only, his
officer's cap commanding the dresser. And remember
your husband's shoulder with its saltier taste here,
outside the marriage bed?

The glass marries silver to serve images, when it
could choose transparency! Never mind. I am
the place where no one lingers. It has made me
ironic. I watch the fanlight over the door as it
wakens, begins to experience day. Light fills it.
A red maple leaf presses there like a warm hand.
Raindrops blown upon it stipple my walls. Such joy—
to reflect on me what it feels. But I am silent.
The inn pattern on my bayberry wallpaper shows a lady
arriving, a coachman cracking his whip. Over and over
she arrives; he departs. Which is as it should be.

III. KITCHEN

Stoop, scrape, ladle, sieve. Rub a lemon against the
silver teeth and it whitens, lets fall its primary color
exuding a fragrance like a cry. A cry in a garden
late at night. I have so much to give—a palette
of color from the shelves: Bell's Seasoning wattled
redgreenyellow like a Van Gogh, a regiment of soup cans.
And spices—pinch them between your fingers, only a pinch.
Who could want more? But at night, when one drop falls
from the faucet, when the refrigerator startles like
a dog dreaming, then I remember the garden: besilvered
broccoli, Kentucky Wonders aloof on their vines.
Children, let me warm you. Preserve you. But they
hold up their stubborn faces, preferring the chill
veils. While from among them a ruffian approaches,
pads up the back steps. Wolf.

ᶴᴇ Legend

God bowls down the heavens and strikes.
The clouds collide with laughter
and Dutchmen cower at the sound it makes.

Each plowboy fears the notorious hereafter:
a penny-dreadful, spelled behind a barn
where batlike angels cluster in the rafters.

Rip sleeps. His young beard whitens beneath stars.
His village stacks up years like firewood.
New Amsterdam grows old. The elms shed hours.

Fool, tell us, was the punchline good
which dizzied you to legend with the gnomes?
Did half-men worship at your hopmad head?

Now the moon's pitying finger crooks you home.
Rip, when you get there, let them know the joke
is earthbound, mulched with dying things. With bones.

~ At 44 Bolton Street

Folks make their own cages
thinks George Featherstone
whose sadness increases
he's so much alone.

He testily sidesteps
the multiple cartons
heaped outside the door
of Miss Emily Martin's

rank, two-room retreat
from which three Siamese
and four alley cats
inspect two shabby trees,

the shelter of children
and home of rude birds
all larking and fighting
at no loss for words—

>   relievo   I got you
>   he's dead   look at me
>   you're it   you're it
>   allee allee in free

Mr. Featherstone's flat
in its bleak precision
is next Mrs. Ryder's
the neighbors' derision

because her lips move
when she halts down the street
strewing crumbs for the birds
who have plenty to eat

since those goddamn dogs
that belong who knows where
tip over the trashcans
the super leaves there.

But all these contentions
the children don't hear
and they're deaf to come-in calls
when summer is near—

              relievo   I got you
              he's dead   look at me
              you're it   you're it
              allee allee in free

If the rent should go up
Mrs. Ryder skips dinner
but mutters: no sparrow
will be any the thinner

if she can help it
and she waits for a letter
and so does Miss Martin
who should know better

and caged Mr. Featherstone
writes to the *News*
and never gets printed
and patches his shoes.

But the mailman gives children
his fat rubber bands
which they snap at the robins
or twang on their hands—

    relievo I got you
    he's dead look at me
    you're it you're it
    allee allee in free

🖋 Mount Auburn Cemetery

Like a dark angel,
the Civil War rode through them,
tearing reserve from their hearts.

   Now marigolds soothe them.

The celibate aunts and uncles
—Greek scholars, birdwatchers—
are granted a field day:
tanager, oriole, indigo bunting.

The young Adelas, Elizas
weave chains of daisies and clematis.
          Under oleander
they whisper at journals. Copy out Whittier,
dare to read Whitman.

So many young wives dead,
      so many babies!

> *He taketh the lambs*
> *In His arms*
> *And carries them*
> *In His bosom.*

Like theirs, our path proves narrow,
the artful edge
      of a ravine. Below, Auburn Lake—
an erotic secret, rippling privately
as mallards idle across it.

The great Bulfinch's tomb
is neglected.
      The large success
of his townsmen
settles into the ground.

At Willow Pond
we lie just touching, aware
of three chaperones benched
across water.

Strict schools
of goldfish appear just below surface,
like insights.

From the Jamesian tower:
dark bronzed trees everywhere,
ringed with the hills
of Chestnut, Somerville, Belmont.

Stairclimbers
call out to each other,
come blinking up into the light.

My arm around you
and a little back from the battlement
we survey our cities.

✎ Rilke Speaks of Angels

From a painting by Lucas van Leyden (1494–1533),
Busch Reisinger Museum.

"Every angel is terrible."
Yet van Leyden's
stands on the crest of a hill

up which the Flemish road
leads like a lesson,

a league perhaps
from a turreted city,
wherein the Virgin bares
her perfect breast

and whiskery St. Anne
offers wine with arthritic fingers.

His broad nostrils,
auburn hair
have about them earth's

comfort, the familiar
bruising
from which millet rises.

And the mouth "so tired, tired"
forbears to speak

lest the wind from God's
"dark book of origins"
ravage the city, scattering
creation like torn embroidery.

From his shoulders grow
great brows,
marked with a creamy white
meadow plumage.

One hand points
protectingly down. The other,
heraldic,
soft-padded at base of thumb,

is a cousin of wings.
"Praise this world
to the Angel. . . . Tell him *things*."

Now the Long Winter

Look, says the cold,
at my frost-ferns, the ornate
and disciplined craft
on your windows.

But we can't see out.
We would rather the clear glass,
though it show us

only the street,
the icebound newspaper.

Stop resisting,
the cold whispers. Let me
enter you like a lover,

bring you my whiteness
that is all colors.

But we want fire—
its flamboyance, the spit
and crackle of logs. We want

flawed, mottled flesh.
Hope runs inside us, hot

as blood,
through as many unlikely channels.

And all we take in,
even you, the cold,
feeds it.

New House

They've left the house open.
There's nothing to steal.
Through the innocent windows
the sun enters on holiday.

Walls the color
of honey and sand.
A clean smell,
sweet as the nape of a neck.

Bricklayers' pollen
motes into air
on a plane of sun.

A juggler
snores in the dining room,
three oranges beside him.

The raftered bedroom
hides lovers,
who wandered here
linked and aching.

Between her legs he traces
whorls like wood shavings.

In the yard, the tissuey trees
are waving, flourishing:

Open your eyes
  to a new light.

Not facts, but the wishes
of everyone passing.

Not furniture,
the geometry of days.

✒ Painting of a Woman with Vines

She lies there, nearly hidden,
except for face and black hair,
in what looks like kudzu.
But she wears it
like bedroom makeshift:
Tuesday's nightgown becoming
the seventh veil. She has
persuaded blue sky
to hang around behind her
and set a peach
on the edge of a cloud
where it streams down nectar.
The stir of her
large, easy body must be
like the gestures of light
over a field. I imagine
toes twitching in dirt
like sparrows.
One thing is certain
and for this I claim her:
she is absolutely swamped
by green, growing things,
but has made of them
an element that suits her.

ʃɭᴇ Landscape with Family

What a harvest. Astonishing.
  You caper like puppies. Ribbon off
across grasses crusted with mountain frost.

          A dappled retriever
camouflages his way to the farmhouse.
The lilt and wheel
  of wild ducks
    enlivens the sky.

Block her! you cry. Or:
  Go down for a pass!
And I fumble—

          Catching
smile of a son, bright cheek
  of his sister, frost against red
    in their father's hair.

Let me stumble, as usual,
  to the wrong goal-line,
butt of your lovejokes.
              For I'm blocked.
        Yes, entirely.
All I would say to you,
              vapor in air.

The mountains stay watchful.
  The sky prepares seasons.
    Over the wasted meadows
      milkweed sails disappear.

◢ Nocturne

A mother goes from room to room, to check on her sleeping
children. She remembers how each first looked to her,
their daily voices, something she said that sprang at
their faces like a slap. There they lie, mouths half open,
as though one would say: "I forgive you." And another:
"Mama, look—the country I travel over is the picture in
The Flying Trunk!" Fireworks, minarets, the tiny sultan
on his balcony. She draws up a blanket, lowers a window.
Outside, the landscape is like the one behind her eyelids
during lovemaking. It stirs, alternately lightens, darkens,
all the while a rushing sound among the austere trees.
A searchlight sweeps over and over the sky: her hands
on her husband's back. His face transformed like the
children's faces, the roofs and trees. All darkened
into themselves, yet illumined. What is he dreaming?
She shivers, catches a glimpse of her dim shape in a child's
mirror. Thinks that she is a night flower in an unvisited
garden. Is the whole family a garden? Larkspur, pansies,
snow-on-the-mountain. And over all the cold stone in the sky,
imagining itself another creature. A pearl diver. Jewel thief.

A NOTE ON THE AUTHOR

Susan Donnelly was born and brought up near Boston. She began writing poetry in 1977, studying with Sam Albert and Harold Bond before forming a workshop of colleagues, Boston & Vicinity, now in its fifth year. Her poems have appeared in *Poetry Northwest*, *Ploughshares*, and *Yankee*, among other magazines and anthologies. She was feature poet in *Soundings East*, an editor of *Dark Horse*, and a second-prize winner in the 1983 Billee Murray Denny national poetry contest. In 1983–84 she held a Hazen Fellowship from Mount Holyoke College. An administrator at Harvard University, she lives in Cambridge with her husband, Kevin. They have a daughter, Rachel, and a son, Patrick.

A NOTE ON THE PRIZE

The Samuel French Morse Poetry Prize was established to honor Professor Morse's distinguished career as teacher, scholar, and poet. Members of the prize committee are: Francis C. Blessington, Joseph deRoche, Susan Goldwitz, Victor Howes, Stuart Peterfreund, and Guy Rotella.

72280200